IMAGES
*of England*

# YORK
## THE SECOND SELECTION

The staff of the lending department of York's first public library in Clifford's Street, in 1895. There was no browsing along the shelves in those days, you had to look for the book you wanted on the indicator which listed all the books available. A member of the staff would then scale a ladder to find it for you.

IMAGES
*of England*

# YORK
## THE SECOND SELECTION

*Compiled by*
Amanda Howard

TEMPUS

First published 1998
Copyright © Amanda Howard, 1998

Tempus Publishing Limited
The Mill, Brimscombe Port,
Stroud, Gloucestershire, GL5 2QG

ISBN 0 7524 1516 6

Typesetting and origination by
Tempus Publishing Limited
Printed in Great Britain by
Midway Clark Printing, Wiltshire

York people extend a warm welcome to Diana, Princess of Wales on her visit with Charles to the National Railway Museum on 12 November 1981.

# Contents

# Acknowledgements

Special thanks to Hugh Murray who shared his extensive knowledge of York with me, to Joe Murphy for his enthusiasm and for allowing me to use many of his photographs and to the City of York Archives for making their collection available to me.

I would like to thank all those who have donated material to the York Central Library in the past. My thanks also to the following, who kindly lent me their own photographs for this book: Avril Appleton, Jane Burrows, Derek Meakin, Mrs N. Paterson, Hilda Robinson, Shepherd Building Group, Jack Wright.

# Introduction

Photographs are an important source for gaining an understanding of the past. The information they contain is immediately accessible; at a glimpse, you are transported into a bygone age and it is possible to obtain an insight into what life used to be like. York Library is fortunate to have built up over the years a collection of over 9,000 illustrations, a substantial number of which are photographs, spanning from the dawn of the photographic age to modern times. They are maintained and preserved in the library and available for everyone to use. The collection has been achieved largely through donations and the library is grateful to those who have entrusted to them their photographs. The majority of the images presented here are from the library's archives, although some have been kindly loaned for the purposes of this book. They demonstrate the range and quality of the archive, which is borne out by the fact that this is a second selection, in which none of the images from the first selection are repeated and many have not been published before.

One aim in selecting the photographs for this book was to choose those that highlight some of the changes that have occurred over the last 150 years. York's reputation as a city steeped in history is well founded and many of the photographs show buildings that survive as a living reminder of its historical past. The skills of the medieval craftsmen are celebrated in the Minster and York's many churches, dating from the Middle Ages, while the antiquity of streets such as Stonegate and The Shambles is renowned. It is easy to imagine when looking at these images that York has been left relatively unmarked by the passage of time. However this impression soon fades when the focus is widened to look beyond the buildings themselves and to encompass the wider city stretching into the suburbs and villages beyond.

Changes in transport are, perhaps, the most noticeable. The streets of Victorian York are full of horses and horse-drawn vehicles, whereas cars now predominate. The replacement of horsepower with motor-driven vehicles not only brought about the alteration of many streets but also contributed to the growth of the suburbs, as it was no longer necessary to live within walking distance of the workplace. Other differences evident from the photographs include the demise of industrial traffic on the rivers, the decline of the military class in society and the transformation of many of the villages around York, which are now included within its boundaries.

Looking through old photographs illustrates just how much of York has altered both dramatically through the demolition of buildings and more subtly in the changes of costume and street furniture. With this in mind and as 1998 has been designated the Year of

Photography, the library has launched the project 'Snap your Street - Now for the Future'. The aim is for all York citizens to take a photograph of their street and donate it to the library, where it will be preserved for future generations as a record of what York looks like as it approaches the millennium. The publication of this book, in the Year of Photography using images taken from the library's collection, is a fitting celebration of the archive that already exists.

# One
# Within the walled city

The Yorkshire Club in Museum Street was draped with bunting in celebration of the Silver Jubilee of George V in 1935.

Spectators flock down Blake Street to watch the Military Sunday Parade wind its way down the road in 1907. Harker's York Hotel juts into St Helens Square making it triangular rather than rectangular as it is today. The hotel started life in 1770 as the York Tavern until Christopher Harker took over the licence in 1850. Its days as one of York's coaching inns came to an end when demolition began in 1928 so that the square could be enlarged.

The buildings between Harker's and Coney Street, facing the Mansion House, in 1928. The narrowness of the road between them and the railings of the Yorkshire Insurance Company offices opposite is evident. When their successors, Barclays Bank and Betty's Café were built, the buildings were smaller and set much further back so that the view from the Mansion House to St Helen's church was uninterrupted.

Laying drains in Stonegate, 14 November 1924. There are several theories as to why Stonegate is so named. Some say that it is because this was the road along which the stone to build the Minster was carried. Others believe that it originates from its medieval paving, while a further possibility is that it dates back to the Roman pavement which is six feet below the present surface level.

Minster Gates with the south door of the Minster making a perfect ending to the street, pictured here in 1959. This transept was badly damaged in the fire of 1984 and from here the blackened Rose Window and the yawning gap between it and the central tower, were clearly visible. The traffic sign in the foreground is a reminder that traffic was allowed down Stonegate and along Petergate with no restrictions until this became York's first pedestrian street in 1971.

High Petergate, *c*. 1905. On the right, Masterman's butchers shop displays the royal arms in support of their dubious claim to have been patronised by Queen Victoria.

Low Petergate in 1925 when it boasted three pubs. The pushchair has just passed the Fox Inn and opposite is the Londesboro' Arms. The third pub is Garrick's Head, close to the junction with Stonegate.

Goodramgate looking towards Petergate, *c.* 1910. Here the buildings are in a bad state of repair. They were drastically 'restored' between 1929 and 1931 when their timbers were exposed. The two shops next to the tallest one, which was Hunter and Smallpage, have now been demolished and replaced by a concrete 1960s structure.

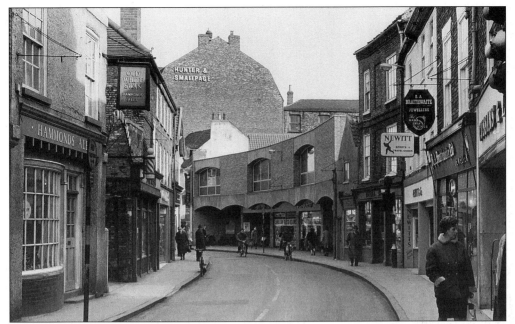

Goodramgate in the late 1960s was home to three long-established York firms, all of which have now moved out. Cussins and Light came to Goodramgate in 1934 but left in 1985 to concentrate their electrical business on their Walmgate store. The furnishers, Hunter and Smallpage opened in 1875 and remained until 1986, when they moved to Micklegate, and Newitts, founded in 1902, closed their sports shop for good in 1995.

King's Square and Petergate, in 1959. The circular flowerbed was a new feature but hardly as impressive as the church of Holy Trinity which had filled the space from the Middle Ages until its demolition in 1937. The premises occupied by Fred Oates the butcher and his neighbours were soon to be sacrificed for one of York's 1960s buildings, the Refuge Assurance shops and office complex.

A lovely view of Holy Trinity in King's Square, from a vantage point outside Audin's fish and chip restaurant, in 1928. It had stood unused for many years before being demolished in 1937 - a victim of its position in the centre of a triangle of medieval churches, St Sampson's in Church Street, Holy Trinity in Goodramgate and St Crux in Pavement.

The junction of three ancient York streets, The Shambles, Newgate and King's Square in the 1950s. King's Square is thought to have been the site of the Palace of the Scandinavian rulers of York (874-954). Newgate was first mentioned in 1328 and The Shambles medieval nature is so famous that, in 1991, the Department of the Environment and the English Tourist Board declared that it was too crowded for people to enjoy!

The Shambles, *c*. 1957. In April 1950, its buildings were scheduled as being of special architectural and historic interest. This prompted a restoration programme and here the soldiers stand in front of a building clad in scaffolding. This was a timely decision; previously the street had been in such a state of disrepair that in November of 1924 a house had actually collapsed.

Market day in St Sampson's Square, 1951. This maintained the long tradition of buying and selling in what used to be called Thursday Market. After Parliament Street was created in 1835-36, the market place stretched from here to Pavement. Its transfer, to the present site in Newgate, was phased in between 1955 and 1964.

The Black Swan in Peaseholme Green, *c.* 1910. Now in splendid isolation, it once had neighbours. The private house has since been incorporated into the pub. On the other side was the Leeds Arms and the entrance to the Haymarket. One of the houses in Haymarket can just be seen on the right hand edge of the photo.

An outing leaves from outside the Black Swan, sometime between 1911 and 1915. The landlord, Fred Wright, was one of the passengers, he poses at the front, holding onto the charabanc. Their destination is unrecorded but wherever it was, the journey must have been uncomfortable with those solid tyres!

Inside Haymarket in 1910. The gas lamp was bracketed to the wall of the Leeds Arms. In the centre of the square is the weighbridge house where the hay was weighed. Above the terraces on the right, the arm of Leetham's flour mill can be seen. It led out into the terraced streets of Hungate, remarkable for their overcrowding and poverty. Today the only reminder of the Haymarket is the car park that bears its name.

The Old George Hotel, 1935. It stood opposite St Crux's parish room. The hotel and its neighbour were demolished to create Stonebow in the early 1950s. The reason for their demolition was to ease the pressure on St Saviourgate which before Stonebow was the only route for traffic to and from Layerthorpe, Heworth and beyond.

The mayoral car is driven down the newly created Stonebow on 14 October 1955. One of the results of this scheme was Stonebow House, voted one of York's ugliest buildings by residents in 1983. It was built in 1960 and is typical of its time - flat, concrete and a break with tradition, all of which make it very conspicuous in a place like York.

The castle complex is seen from the air on 2 July 1926. This shows it to be enclosed by an impressive curtain wall. The imposing gateway opposite Clifford's Tower was the entrance into the law court area. The governor's house is at the other side of Clifford's Tower and radiating from it are the cell blocks of the male prison. In the foreground is the debtors' prison. To its left are the civil and criminal courts and to the right the female prison. The governor's house and male prison were demolished in 1935 and the site is now the castle car park, while the debtors' prison and female prison now house the Castle Museum.

The gardens in Tower Street in the shadow of the curtain wall, *c.* 1900. The walls surrounding the castle area were built of grey gritstone and were very imposing. When they were demolished in 1935, the stone was reused for different purposes, including road widening and in the building of boundary walls for the new housing developments that were underway in the 1930s in Stockton Lane and Rawcliffe.

Clifford's Tower and the castle yard, seen from within the castle walls. The large turreted building is the governor's house, where the families of the governor and the deputy governor and other members of the prison staff lived. Stretching from the back of the governor's house to the spire of St Mary's is one of the long, thin cell blocks of the male prison. The wall separated the prison from the law courts.

Clifford Street in the early 1940s. Unusually for York all the architecture is of a similar age and style. This is because the whole street had been created between 1880 and '82. Before this, the three lanes; First, Middle and Far Water Lane stretched from the river up to Castlegate. They were notorious for their unsanitary and overcrowded conditions and were the only slums to be cleared in the nineteenth century.

Nessgate, 7 December 1903. This row of shops, stretching from King Street to Low Ousegate, was about to be demolished so that the road could be widened in preparation for the anticipated arrival of the electric trams. A single building, set much further back, replaced these five. It was the Coach and Horses public house, locally known as the Big Coach.

Looking towards Ousegate from Ouse Bridge, 1890. There is hardly a break in the row of buildings along the right hand side of the street with Nessgate emerging into Low Ousegate through a very narrow opening. This changed in 1905 when the corner was widened as part of the Nessgate improvement scheme.

J. Backhouse and Son at the corner of Bridge Street and George Hudson Street shortly after it opened on 19 June 1905. Backhouses' nursery and seed business was long established in York and they had a world famous reputation for, among other feats, pioneering the cultivation of alpine plants. Their nurseries at Holgate attracted many visitors and West Bank Park is their legacy to York people today.

A horse and cart stand on the cobbles of North Street, c. 1880. At this time it was an area of closely packed terraced streets and courts. The spire of All Saints church rises over the rooftops. This corner is now dominated by the new General Accident office block.

The approach to the newly constructed Lendal Bridge, *c.* 1870. Rougier Street is just a narrow lane and opposite there is no Station Road. The walls have not yet been breached so that the only way out of the city on this side, between Micklegate and Bootham Bars, is through North Street postern. Behind the high wall, railway vehicles stand on the sidings from the station which, at this time, was within the walls in Toft Green.

# Two
# Without the walls

A tram carries its passengers along Gillygate at sometime between 1910 and 1916. Virtually empty of traffic then, today it is one of York's busiest streets.

Pedestrians of all ages can be seen at the junction of Haxby Road, Wigginton Road, Clarence Street , Union Terrace and Lowther Street, *c.* 1900. The Punch Bowl on the corner of Lowther Street has been there since the mid-1850s, at which time the terraces started to grow up around it.

Mixed expressions on the faces of Lowther United football team, 1907.

RENCE GARDENS
HAXBY ROAD, YORK

W. Hayes
Photo.

Clarence Gardens, 1904. This area between Haxby Road and Wigginton Road was traditionally used for fairs and was known as Horsefair. The park opened on 19 May 1902 and was initially called The Haxby Road Recreation Ground. It was renamed two months later as Clarence Gardens, after the Duke of Clarence who had been awarded the honorary freedom of York. Their claim to fame is that they were home to the first municipal bowling green in the city, which opened in 1908.

A steam train passes the Burton Lane signal box on its way to Scarborough in the 1930s. The level crossing was at the junction of Field View and Burton Stone Lane. The signalman is just leaving his box. His days were numbered, however, as the crossing was about to be replaced by the new bridge, as pictured opposite.

The new bridge which carries Crichton Avenue over the London and North Eastern Railway line was under construction in the 1930s. When it was completed the Field View crossing was closed.

Troops of the York and Lancaster Regiment guard the level crossing at Field View during the railway strike in 1911. It was a nationwide strike over union recognition as well as pay and conditions. This was a year of great industrial tension in York with the workers at Leetham's flour mill, the Ebor flour mill and York glassworks all striking. Even the school children at Queen Street School went on a short-lived strike for less homework, cushioned seats and fewer beatings!

Garth Terrace off Burton Stone Lane, *c.* 1910. In the 1902 directory only eight houses are listed, though it states that a further eight were being built. By the time the 1909 directory was published the street had been finished. Much of the housing in the Burton Stone Lane area developed following the opening of the Rowntree's factory on Haxby Road.

Clifton residents, *c.* 1905. Clifton did not become a part of York until 1884. This integration faced some opposition from those who wished to retain its independent township status.

Three boys from St Peter's row out to rescue two damsels in distress, stranded on the fence around Clifton Green during the severe floods of March 1947.

A bonfire on Clifton Green. To its right is a pair of cottages standing on what is now the entrance to Water Lane. Hopefully they won't be adding a guy to the bonfire - Guy Fawkes is an old boy of St Peter's School, only a stone's throw away, where the burning of guys is now against the school rules!

The bailey bridge over the River Ouse at Clifton, in 1961. It was erected as a temporary measure to cope with the extra traffic generated by the marriage of Katherine Worsley to the Duke of Kent, which took place in York Minster. This proved that there was a need for a bridge here and the present bridge was opened in October 1963. Before this the only way across the river was by ferry at Clifton Scrope.

The helter skelter, one of the many attractions on offer at The Grand York Gala and Flower Show, held in the grounds of Bootham Hospital. The show was held annually from its inauguration in 1858 until 1934. Its purpose was threefold - to raise money for local charities, to provide a forum for exhibiting flowers and produce and to entertain visitors.

A fresh produce display at the York Gala in 1909. Items were shown in a number of categories; plants, cut flowers, table decorations, hand baskets, bouquets, fruit and vegetables. Prizes were awarded to the best entrants, ranging from £20 for a large display of miscellaneous plants to 10s for a dish of cherries.

YORK GALA.

The York Gala in the grounds of Bootham hospital, 21 June 1906. Fairground rides, stage performances from acrobats, clowns and trapeze artists, a full programme of music given by military bands and at dusk, a firework display were among the events at the gala in this year.

Hot air balloon rides were also a popular feature. Certificates of ascent were presented to those who dared and courage was certainly required after a balloon broke free in 1911 and drifted for an hour and a half before coming down in a tree near Elvington, seven miles from York!

Bootham Bar, c. 1881. This is one of the most photographed scenes in York, but unlike many others, this time a view through Queen Mary's Arch to Wilson's shop has been included. John Eden Wilson is recorded in the 1881-82 directory as a linen draper at No. 2 Bootham. He later moved to Pavement taking the shop sign with him. The ironwork structure behind the waiting cab, is a men's public convenience which was open aired. When the steps were added to the bar in 1889, the structure had to be roofed over for the sake of decency!

York Lifeboat Procession makes its way along Queen Street on 8 July 1899. The lifeboat is *The Bushie*, which had saved thirty-three lives, and the aim of the day was to raise funds for the Royal National Lifeboat Institution. Also in the parade were marching bands, civic dignitaries and the three emergency services. The day was blessed by fine weather and large crowds turned out to witness the spectacle.

Holgate Road Railway Bridge under construction in 1911. This was the third bridge here and had to be built to bear the weight of the newly installed electric trams. Until the bridge opened in August 1911, passengers travelling to and from Acomb had to leave their tram at one side of the bridge, cross on foot and board another tram to take them on the second leg of their journey.

The tram stops at the boundary of York and Acomb in 1911. It stands between what are now the Regent Buildings and Oak Haven Old People's Home. There was a proposal in 1913 to extend the tramlines into Acomb itself but it was strongly opposed by many residents, in the belief that it would lead to them paying York's higher rates, and was consequently dropped.

Two minis pass each other in Front Street, Acomb in 1965. On the right is Acomb Primary School. It opened in August 1894 with 230 pupils on the register, but only four teachers. Lack of space forced the school to move to larger premises in 1995 and their former accommodation is being converted into shops. The long, low roof next door is the Acomb Methodist Assembly Hall.

Front Street, Acomb and the junction with Carr Lane in the late 1920s. The development of the Carr Lane estate shifted the focus of Acomb to here, from its traditional centre around the green and along the road where the library now stands. The row of terraces, where they have survived, have been converted into shops and now form Acomb's main shopping street.

The pupils of Dringhouses School in St Helens Road. There has been a school in Dringhouses since 1849. Originally housed in a school room next to the church, it later moved to the buildings now occupied by Dringhouses Library. It opened in St Helens Road in 1904 and is still there today.

The corner of Albemarle Road in June 1922, before it was widened. This was called South Mount Terrace and the house is now the Mount Royale Hotel. The photograph was taken by the city librarian, Albert Finney, who regularly photographed streetscapes that were about to be altered to add to the library's collection.

The workers at Terry's factory on Bishopthorpe Road greet King George VI and Queen Elizabeth on 19 October 1937. The visit coincided with the 270th anniversary of the foundation of the firm and they were prosperous times. In 1920 a new chocolate production block had been built at their Clementhorpe site and, in 1926, building was underway at their new Bishopthorpe Road factory.

Victorian terraces and Southlands Wesleyan chapel on Bishopthorpe Road, *c.* 1919. The chapel was built in 1886 and is still in use today. Southlands marks the extent to which the Victorian expansion behind Bishopthorpe Road reached. The land beyond Southlands was left for the developers of the 1930s to utilise.

Mr Paterson with his class of boys at St Clements School in Cherry Street, *c.* 1905. The school opened in May 1872 in Cherry Street and children of the area were educated here until it closed in August 1960.

Mr Paterson with his class at St Clement's School about thirty years later. He must have witnessed many changes in his teaching career. His class is smaller and there are now girls as well as boys. The uniform has gone and so has the formality of earlier times.

The funeral procession of Lord Mayor William Bently crosses Castle Mills Bridge on 4 February 1907. He had lived in Fulford Grange where he had held many charitable events. He died in office at the age of only 53 years. The crowds lining the street are evidence that he was well known and liked in the city.

Sandringham Street, *c*. 1893. The shop on the corner was a baker and confectioners belonging to Thomas Tittensor. The 1891 census returns reveal that several residents in the street worked at the nearby glassworks and gave their occupations as glass bottle maker, glass cutter and engraver.

F. Shepherd and Son's steam wagon outside their premises in Blue Bridge Lane in 1925. Originally running their building business from Lead Mill Lane in Walmgate, the company moved to Blue Bridge Lane in 1927 and still operates in the Fulford Road area. They have just built a prestigious new office complex, Fulfordmoor House, which reflects their success.

A garden party in the grounds of Kilburn House, Fulford Road in July 1913. The host was Alderman Joseph Agar who was aged 80 at the time and had held the office of Lord Mayor three times. The house was built in the early nineteenth century and demolished following Agar's death in 1920. Several streets including Kilburn Road have now been built on the site.

The residents of Kent Street, at a time when houses occupied the area rather than a car park, are given rides by Mr Dennison, a chimney sweep from March Street. He also entertained the children with a roundabout that he cranked by hand.

Cows await their fate in the pens at York Cattlemarket in 1964. The cattle market with its twin cupolas was built in 1826 and was regularly added to until its closure in February 1964 following a move to Murton. The Barbican Centre now stands here. It must have been a lively place with the cow 'wallopers' driving cattle along the approach roads, farmers inspecting the animals and auctioneers controlling the bids. In addition there were all the refreshment stalls and pubs that quenched the thirst of the workers.

Walmgate Bar is seen from Lawrence Street showing the Barbican. It was badly damaged in the civil war and again more recently. This time, however, the damage was caused by lorries getting wedged under the arch rather than warring soldiers! The scene can be precisely dated from the billboard announcing a fire at Selby Abbey, which occurred on 19 October 1906.

DECORATED REGENT ST DURING JUBILEE CELEBRATION WEEK 1935.

Regent Street was decorated for the jubilee celebration week in 1935. This terraced street and others like it used to stretch between Lawrence Street and Heslington Road, but were cleared only two years later in 1937. After the site had lain empty for nearly four decades, thirty-two 'instant bungalows' were erected there in 1976.

The crossroads of Lawrence Street, Hull Road, Melrosegate and Green Dykes Lane, c. 1930. Part of the emerging Tang Hall estate can be seen in the distance, though the 1930s semi's have not yet appeared opposite the black and white building. This was branch No. 31 of the Co-op, which opened in 1929. The houses on the corner of Lawrence Street are still there today but are almost unrecognisable as part of Tang Hall Working Men's Club.

Children enjoy Hull Road Park shortly after it opened in 1928.

Flooding at the junction of Melrosegate and Fourth Avenue in Tang Hall in March 1947. This was a year in which severe flooding occured throughout the city.

A quiet East Parade, Heworth, c. 1900. The spire belongs to Holy Trinity church which was designed by the York architect George Fowler Jones in 1868. At first it stood alone on this side of the road, until terraces filled both sides. Heworth Methodist chapel, built in 1890, can just be seen on the horizon.

This view of Elmfield College was probably captured for its jubilee year in 1914. It had been founded as a Primitive Methodist boarding school in 1864 and educated boys to live up to the standard of 'plain living and high learning' until it closed in 1932. Only the house on the right is still standing today in Straylands Grove, the rest were demolished to make way for the Elmpark estate, Heworth Rugby Club and York Cricket Club.

John R. Hayes' corner shop in 1902. Although Mill Lane was written on the hand cart, it was actually on the corner of Harcourt Street, opposite London's newsagent and toyshop in Heworth. The building now houses a branch of the Halifax bank.

Downhill Street in Layerthorpe, which led onto the banks of the River Foss. Its small, narrow terraces were typical of the Layerthorpe area. However, the cramped conditions did not prevent small businesses developing and J.T.P. Giles operated his coal business from his home here in the 1920s and early '30s.

The staff of the Layerthorpe Co-op stand outside their shop in 1916. The Equitable Industrial Society, which became the Co-operative Society, had branches throughout the country in the poorer areas of the community. York's first store opened in 1889 in Holgate Road where housing was developing for the growing number of railway workers and their families.

Monk Bridge, c. 1902. A fatal accident occurred here when the bridge was being rebuilt in 1794 for the Foss Navigation. The keystone in the centre gave way and the whole structure collapsed, instantly killing one workman and seriously injuring the other. A subscription was raised for their families and within a week a considerable sum had amassed.

Reinforced concrete was used to widen Monk Bridge in June 1925. The extra arch was added next to the 1794 stone arch. The photograph was taken at 5p.m., the labourers are still hard at work while those on their way home stop to watch their progress.

There was an elephant parade along Monkgate when the circus came to town in 1908.

Lord Mayor's Walk looked like a country lane at the turn of the century and cyclists could pedal along in the middle of the road without worrying about the traffic that is continually present today.

# *Three*
# Along the rivers

Barges on the Ouse, *c.* 1905. Rivers were the motorways of the age, used for carrying both finished goods and raw materials. Archaeological evidence has proved that from the earliest times, industry has congregated along river banks. Many York businesses started life on riverside sites.

To the right of Lendal Bridge is Rowntree's factory. Rowntree's Cocoa Works started life here in North Street in 1861. Even after the move to the Haxby Road site, they maintained a presence here. Their warehouse was a casualty of the Baedeker raid of 29 April 1942.

A horse stands outside Rowntree's North Street factory waiting to take away the results of a day's work, c. 1880. For many years it was a small-scale industry with Joseph Rowntree himself making cocoa and confectionery in the factory. Mr Laycock stands by the rulley. He collected from Rowntree for the North Eastern Railways from 1877 until his death in 1911.

Blundy's Yard overlooking the river in North Street 1911. A barge is standing ready to receive its load. Blundy's was a coal, sand and gravel merchants established in 1912. They had substantial premises on the riverside.

The offices of Blundy, Clark and Co. in North Street, c. 1940. In 1962 they merged with Chadwick Hardgreaves of Scarborough and a year later these offices were closed and the company moved to Micklegate.

Traditional forms of transport, *c.* 1890. The cargo of a barge is unloaded onto the cart under Skeldergate Bridge.

Terry's factory in Clementhorpe in 1973, shortly before it was demolished. Originally they manufactured in St Helen's Square but moved here in 1864. At this time they were famous for candied peel, medicated lozenges and other sweets. Cocoa and chocolate production didn't start until 1886.

Workers in the Lozenge Department of Terry's, outside the starch room at Clementhorpe. This is a reminder of the fact that child labour was commonly used in factories in the Victorian age. The picture includes Frank Lowther who started work here in 1889 at the age of 12 or 13 and stayed until he retired in 1941 at the age of 65.

Henry Richardson and Co. on the banks of the Ouse, in the 1940s. The company was founded in 1824 and produced fertilisers for the surrounding farming areas. Manufacture ceased following their merger with Anderton's of Howden in July 1958 and in 1967 the company was taken over by Hardgreaves Fertilisers.

Redfearn's National Glass Company dominated Castle Mills Bridge in 1954. Glass manufacture was a long-established trade in this area, stretching back to the 1790s. In 1930, Redfearns stepped in to carry on a tradition that ended with their closure in 1983. The Novotel now occupies this site.

Empty barges stand in Browney Dyke on the Foss beyond Castle Mills Bridge, sometime between 1905 and 1910. They await their cargo from the glassworks or one of the other firms who used the river to transport their goods.

The new Castle Mills Bridge under construction in July 1956. It replaced the earlier bridge which had become too narrow for the increasing amount of traffic that crossed it everyday. It was officially opened on 23 November 1956 by Hugh Molson from the Ministry of Transport.

Leetham's flour mills on the River Foss in August 1912. The mill was founded by Henry Leetham in 1850 and rapidly expanded in the 1880s and 1890s. It made full use of its riverside position, with flour and grain soon replacing coal as the main river traffic. In 1911, the milling industry accounted for 600 jobs in York but the work was hard. Workers were poorly paid, often endured twelve hour shifts and spent much of their time heaving heavy sacks.

Garden Place, 1910. The silos and conveyor of Leetham's mill were a visible presence on the skyline of York until its closure in 1930. The mill dominated the streets of Hungate and many of the workers came from here and nearby Walmgate and Layerthorpe. The only reminder of the mill today is Rowntree's Wharf, now converted to flats. Rowntree acquired it in 1937, after the mill closed in 1930.

These strange looking conical shapes stood on Wormalds's Cut in 1912. They were used at Leetham's mill and inverted, spun round to draw the flour dust out of the atmosphere. This was important as it was highly combustible and the mill suffered two fires in its history.

GREAT FIRE AT MILL'S MILL YORK.
APRIL 7.11. 6 AM

Water is sprayed from the fire fighting tug, the Sir Joseph Rymer, in an attempt to contain the flames on C.D. Mills premises in 1911. They had milled flour in Skeldergate since the 1860s but increased competition from national firms forced them out of business in 1936.

The fire fighters take a rest by Skeldergate Bridge after finally putting out the fire at Mill's mill in 1911.

The River King at King's Staith in 1905. Although the river was heavy with industrial traffic, there was still time for pleasure craft, this one would be taking passengers for a trip along the river to Bishopthorpe or Nun Monkton. In January 1777 King's Staith was the scene for attempts by a press gang to capture men for military service.

Spectators sit on the steps of the York City Rowing Club, on the south of the Ouse, to watch a regatta. In recent times the rivers have ceased to be an industrial highway. The last commercial use was by the Yorkshire Evening Press, who had their paper delivered by boat.

Fishing under Lendal Bridge. The river frontage along the Ouse is one of York's assets. Without the presence of industrial river traffic, the river can be enjoyed for its beauty and used for recreation.

# Four

# At worship

An aerial view of York, in August 1935. The Minster dominates with its sheer size and the towers of five of York's many parish churches can be seen. There were forty-six churches in medieval York and of these eighteen have survived. Since the Middle Ages, churches and chapels have continued to appear in the city centre and the expanding suburbs.

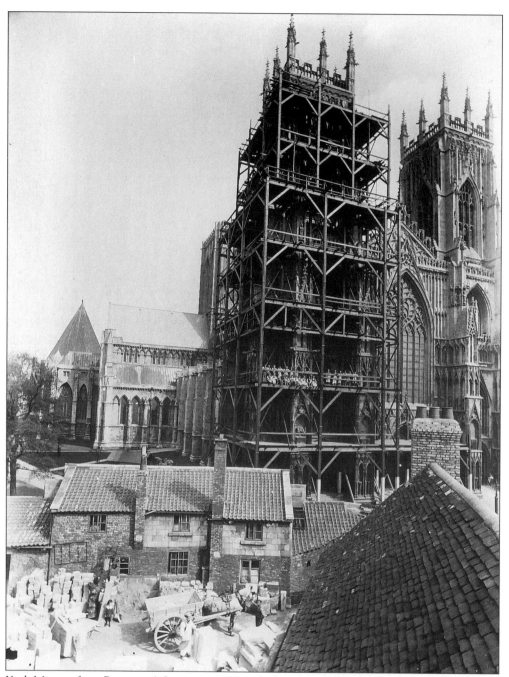

York Minster from Precentor's Lane pre-1919 with the stoneyard in the foreground. Scaffolding on the Minster is not an unusual sight! In 1921 the dean reported to the chapter, as have many deans before and after him, that although the fabric was generally in a good state, repairs were always ongoing. Here the scaffolding is wooden and the workers don't appear to have taken any safety precautions.

The staff responsible for the upkeep of the fabric of the Minster are pictured outside the new stoneyard in Deangate on 17 February 1914. There were seven masons, one carver, three joiners, one bricklayer, six labourers and three policemen. The bearded officer is Sergeant Morley and next to him is R.C. Green, the Clerk of the Works who was in overall charge.

Restoration work on York Minster windows, *c.* 1923. An appeal was launched in November 1920 to raise money for the restoration of the windows. Awareness of their poor condition was brought about during, and as a result of, the First World War when twenty-one windows were taken out and buried in the ramparts of the city walls following the threat of enemy bombing raids. A further effect of the war was that it raised the cost of labour and materials, such as lead, to almost double their pre-war prices.

Workmen carry out the essential task of cleaning and releading the windows in 1923. The Minster has the finest and largest collection of medieval stained glass in the world. Over time the lead can become warped, bent, perished or may peel off. The window then becomes distorted and bulges so that the glass can crack or fall out.

Masons repair the exterior stonework in the 1920s. Below them is The Old Deanery, which was built in 1834 for Dean Cockburn. It was demolished in 1937 when the current deanery was completed. Behind the deanery is the former Archbishop's Palace, now the Minster Library.

The Minster bell ringers face the camera for a photograph to mark the first recording of the peal on disc, by HMV, in February 1928.

A beautiful view of the remaining wall of the medieval Archbishop's Palace in Dean's Park, with a gardener and tree in silhouette. The wall was restored in 1987 as a memorial to the soldiers of the 2nd Division. It commemorates the battles they have fought, from their first in Portugal in 1809 to the World War Two battles of Mandalay and Rangoon.

St Crux church in Pavement, *c.* 1880. The hanging sheep outside the Golden Fleece and the double gable of Thomas Herbert's house are the only recognisable features today. An Italian-style tower topped with a cupola gives it a different appearance to the other surviving churches in York. It was, however, found to be unsafe in 1872 and was consequently demolished.

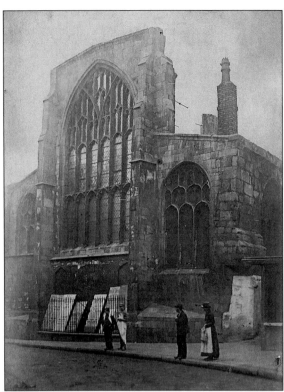

St Crux stood partly demolished between 1884 and 1887 while moves were made to save it. A restoration appeal had been launched in 1883, to raise the money required for rebuilding, but sadly time ran out. It was finally destroyed in 1887.

The devastation of St Crux from the interior, 1884. Some of the monuments from inside were saved and put into St Crux parish room, which replaced the church.

St Sampson's church, 1955. Services had stopped here in 1949, but it received a new lease of life when it was converted, by The Civic Trust, into a meeting place for old people. It was officially opened by the Queen Mother on 13 November 1974 and she is reported to have 'laughed and talked with nearly everyone invited.'

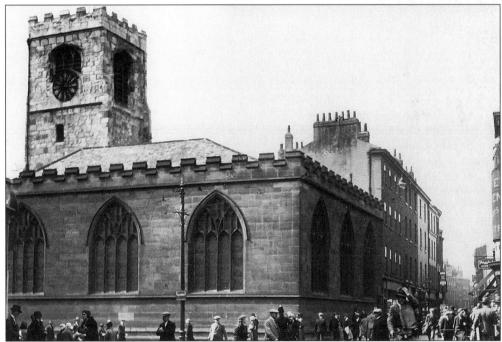

St Michael Spurriergate is another of York's medieval churches that is now used for another purpose – a thriving café and Christian centre. Here in 1932, it still had its tower where the curfew bell was traditionally rung every night at 8p.m. – a practice that occurred as late as 1931. It was removed in 1968 and the clock was fixed to the wall where it remains today.

St John's church in Micklegate looked different in the 1880s when it had a churchyard surrounded by railings. This was lost in 1965 when the street was widened. The row of shops next to it also went as part of the scheme. In the 1930s it was one of a group of medieval churches on the hit list for demolition. It closed in 1939, but was reprieved and is now the Arts Centre.

St Martin Le Grand in Coney Street, complete with both aisles, before it was damaged in the Baedeker raid of 29 April 1942. The parts that survived were restored and it was rehallowed in April 1968 as a memorial to the York citizens killed in the two World Wars. The clock is a useful landmark for shoppers in Coney Street. There has been a clock here since 1668. The famous figure on top, the little admiral, was added about 100 years later.

Workmen taking a break lean against the wall of St Cuthbert's. On the gable end wall, the outline where another building butted up against it can clearly be seen. Today it is hidden behind trees.

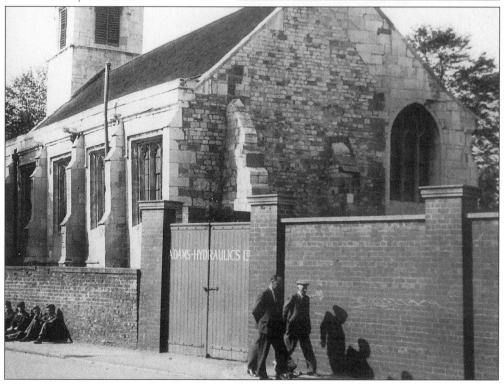

St Cuthbert's Sunday School Concert 1910-1919. Revd Pyne, the tall man on the back row, was well loved by his parishioners. He is remembered for his kindness and generosity and particularly for his involvement with the young people of the parish at the boys and girls school, the Sunday school and the Boys Club.

Goats tethered to a tree in the churchyard of St Saviour's. Using the churchyard for pasture was a long-established custom. As well as providing food for the animals, it ensured that the grass remained short.

A group of children enjoy a picnic in the churchyard of Holy Trinity Goodramgate, in 1890. One hundred years later, it is still a good place for a picnic. Its secluded off-street position gives it a feeling of peace and antiquity. This is mirrored inside the church, whose interior is one of the few to have escaped a Victorian restoration. It is maintained by the Churches Conservation Trust.

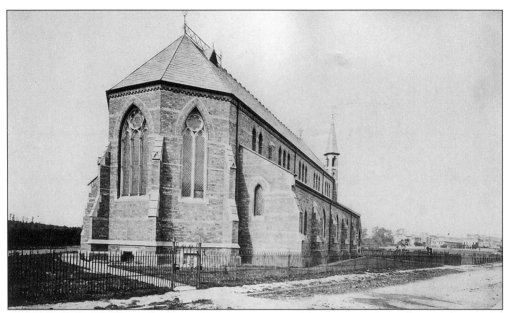

St Clement's on Scarcroft Road, newly built in 1874 and to modern eyes strangely isolated. Its presence is a testament to how far the growth of the suburbs to the south of York had reached. In the 1872 Street Directory, Russell Street, Thorpe Street and Millfield Road are not listed. By 1924, the suburb had extended so far beyond St Clement's that another church, St Chad's, was built.

Christ Church, Heworth was built for the new housing estates growing up off Stockton Lane in the 1960s. Here in October 1963, the very modern fibre-glass spire, standing 35 feet high and weighing 1.5 tons, is about to be lifted on. The church was completed with amazing speed - the first turfs were cut in April 1963 and the dedication service was held in March 1964.

St Mary's Bishophill Junior and St Columba's are seen from the bar walls, 1908. This area is remarkable for the number of places of worship it contains. The two Anglican churches of St Mary and Holy Trinity on Micklegate sandwich a trio of non-conformist chapels representing the Wesleyians, the Baptists and the Presbyterians.

The most prolific builders of churches and chapels in the nineteenth and twentieth centuries were the non-conformists. This is the bricklaying ceremony of the Central Mission's new hall in Swinegate in April 1910. It is now the York Elim church.

The Salem chapel, at the end of St Saviourgate, built for the Congregationalists in 1839. It could seat 2,000 people but in the 1930s was rarely used. It was demolished in 1964 and replaced by Hilary House, a typical '60s office block.

STONE LAYING
CLIFTON WESLEYAN CHURCH

A family day out at the Clifton Weslyan stone laying ceremony in May 1908. The Wesleyans in particular were quick to open chapels in the developing suburbs. These foundations grew into the large red brick chapel that stands opposite the Burton Stone Inn. It opened on 10 November 1909.

A cradle rally at Victoria Bar Primitive Methodist chapel on 1 July 1923. All of the children are beautifully presented in their Sunday best, although given some of their expressions, it is not certain that they are all enjoying the service! The chapel was active from 1880 to 1940 but has since been converted into flats.

St Wilfrid's Roman Catholic church in Duncombe Place, 1864-1869. When the church opened in 1864, there could have been little doubt about what it would be called. There was medieval St Wilfrid's church close to the present one, a Mission of St Wilfrid was founded in Little Blake Street in 1742 and in 1802 a chapel dedicated to the saint opened where the church stands today. The house that juts out was demolished in 1883 prior to the building of the Probate Registry.

The church and presbytery of English Martyrs Roman Catholic church in Dalton Terrace, 1941. Work had begun in 1931 and its simple lines reflect the style of the period. It was the first in a spate of Roman Catholic foundations in the suburbs. The original St Aelred's opened in Tang hall in 1932, worship began at St Joseph's in Clifton in 1939 and Our Lady's in Acomb was completed in 1955.

The Roman Catholic Guild of Our Lady of Ransom process down Museum Street on the way to the Tyburn on the Knavesmire where fifty-two martyrs were executed.

*Five*

# The transport revolution

A horse and carriage passes the castle walls in Tower Street in a scene evocative of a period drama film set.

Hansom cabs were a familiar sight on the streets of Victorian England and can be easily identified by their large wheels and the driver standing at the back holding onto long reins. Here the cab is approaching St Martin Le Grand in Coney Street. It is particularly fitting that there is a photograph of one in York as their inventor, Joseph Aloysius Hansom, had lived in Micklegate.

Two carriages pass each other in Blake Street, c. 1903. Blake Street would have been packed with carriages, their occupants attending functions at the Assembly Rooms during their heyday in the eighteenth century. So much so that, in 1745, the graveyard of St Helen's was removed to allow carriages to pass more easily. Street widening has a long history in York as the narrow medieval streets have been adapted to cater for different needs.

A horse-drawn tram at the corner of Micklegate and George Hudson Street, in 1905. The man in the flat cap is leading the trace horse, which waited at the bottom of Micklegate Hill. It was attached to the tramcar to help the horses to pull the tram up the hill.

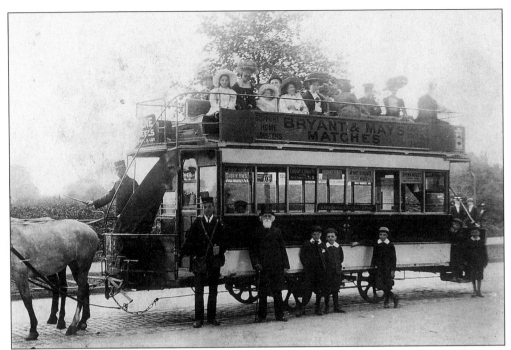

A posed photograph of the last of the horse-drawn trams in York, in 1909. They had been a familiar sight on the streets of York since 1880 but in 1909 were about to be replaced by the latest technology – electric trams.

Workers lift the horse tram tracks in Blossom Street in 1909 ready for the narrow gauge tracks of the electric trams to be laid.

The tracks for the electric trams are put in place at the junction of The Mount and Holgate Road in 1909. Wooden boards rested on the rails to allow pedestrians to cross Holgate Road.

York's first electric tramcar, pictured in Clifford Street in January 1910. It ran from Fulford to Nessgate and, after all the upheaval of the preparations, was enthusiastically received by the crowds who lined the streets to watch it. The trams were a familiar sight on York streets until the last one ran in November 1935, by which time they had been superseded by motor buses.

Queen Street in 1907 was a much narrower street than it is today. It was just about to be widened for the anticipated arrival of the electric trams.

Street widening has begun by 23 July 1907. The casualty was J.R. Swales, a fine art dealer, carver and gilder. Brown Bros and Taylor, furnishers, advertise their business while they can in the windows. Its neighbour, the Windmill pub was spared and now forms the corner of Blossom Street and Queen Street.

Men are at work strengthening Lendal Bridge to take the weight of the trams in 1910. Extra steel ribs were installed to ensure that the bridge would bear the weight of the trams.

Trams in Nessgate, c. 1920 – or is it an advertisement for Heinz! Championed by one tram are baked beans in tomato sauce, while the other promotes tomato ketchup.

A tram waits at the Haxby Road terminus, which opened in June 1910. The line was extended to Rowntree's factory when the bridge over the railway on Haxby Road was strengthened in 1916. Tramlines extending into the suburbs were an important factor in their development.

Buses wait at the station in 1941. Buses had operated side by side with electric trams in the city since 1915. This lasted until November 1935 when the last tram was seen on the streets of York. The motor buses had triumphed over them as a result of their ability to reach the expanding suburbs without the need for tramlines and cables.

A busy scene on the platform of York station, *c.* 1908. The station had opened in June 1877 and was accorded high praise in the *Yorkshire Gazette*. It stated that, 'never since the building of the glorious Minster centuries ago had so immense and noble a structure reared its head in York'! By 1908 there were 352 trains per day running through York and about 6,000 people were employed in the railway industry there. York's importance as a railway centre was such that the trains of seven mainline companies were using the station.

A train pulls into York station, *c.* 1910. The arrival of the railways had an enormous impact on the city. They were a major employer, they stimulated the expansion of other local industries and the location of the carriage works in Holgate transformed it into a large suburb and impacted on the growth of Acomb. Additionally, the sheer size of the buildings they necessitated – the station, hotel and the NER offices – changed the complexion of York.

The Station Hotel seen from the North Eastern Railway offices, *c.* 1906. This opened a year after the station, in 1878. The size of the building is amazing and one explanation for this is that it was designed to hide the railway lines and workings of the station. Another theory is that it was to reassure investors of the solidity and permanence of the railways. However, with the increased number of visitors the railways brought to York, it was not too big for its needs and in fact, it was extended in 1894.

The North Eastern Railway offices when newly constructed in 1906. Their size and grandeur reflect the confidence of the company at the time. In front, dwarfed by the new building, are the tram sheds of the old station. This was York's second station, opening in 1840. Part of the old station continued to be used as offices despite the size of the purpose-built ones. This has ensured that at least some of the old station buildings have survived.

Looking through the walls to the statue of George Leeman in 1905. The walls were cut through in 1874-6 prior to the opening of the station in 1877 to provide access to it from Lendal Bridge. The statue of Leeman, an influential figure in York's railway history, was unveiled in April 1885 and was created by the York sculptor G.W. Milburn.

A lone car drives through Monk Bar in the 1920s. Increasing traffic volume fifty years later threatened to sweep away what is now Bulmers (to the right of the bar), the pub opposite and its neighbour. In 1971, a compulsory purchase order was placed on them so that the junction could be improved and an up to date traffic signalling system installed. Although the house next to the pub was pulled down, the others were saved following public protest

A portent for the future as cars begin to outnumber more traditional modes of transport in Blossom Street, *c.* 1920.

Motor traffic fills the road in front of Micklegate Bar in the 1960s. A transport revolution has occurred.

Cars, delivery vans and pedestrians in Coney Street in the early 1940s. There has recently been a change in attitude towards vehicular access to the streets in the city centre. In the past cars, and previously trams, were given priority and buildings were pulled down where they stood in the way. Today traffic needs are balanced with the need to preserve York's historic architecture and to provide a safe and pleasant environment. Stonegate was pedestrianised in 1971, but the footstreets scheme did not truly get underway until 1986-7.

*Six*

# Military associations

The bar walls are a visible reminder of York's military past. Parts of the Roman wall were incorporated into the foundations of the medieval wall. They fully enclosed the city in the reigns of Edward I and III to protect it from Scottish invasion and they were needed during the civil war. Since then however they have been maintained more for civic pride than military necessity.

St Lawrence's church, 1854. This was damaged during a Parliamentarian attack on Walmgate Bar in the civil war. The Parliamentarians besieged the city in the summer of 1644 but the Royalists hung on until their defeat at the Battle of Marston Moor on 2 July. It was eventually repaired after the war and stood until 1883 when the new St Lawrence's was built. The tower and doorway remain in the churchyard.

St Mary's Tower in Bootham, *c.* 1907. On 16 June 1644, the tower was blown up when the Parliamentarians breached the city's defences and reached King's Manor, where the King had his northern headquarters. After a bloody skirmish they were beaten back by the Royalists. When the tower was restored, it was considerably smaller. Now that the adjoining buildings have been knocked down, the line of the original wall can be seen.

Two passers by watch the Yorkshire Hussars changing guard at the cavalry barracks on Fulford Road, *c.* 1900. The barracks were built between 1794 and 1795 with enough room for 261 men and 266 horses. The infantry barracks were erected further down Fulford Road in 1877-80. Together they gave York a distinctive military character.

The band of the Yorkshire Hussars in 1900. They would have looked splendid in their blue serge uniforms, embellished with gold braid.

Cabs wait outside The Barrack Tavern in Fulford Road, 1880-1885. The tavern was virtually guaranteed to be successful when it started trading next door to the cavalry barracks in 1801. It is still a pub today, although the name has been changed to The Fulford Arms.

Two photographers stand on step ladders in Duncombe Place to capture the splendour of the Military Sunday parade in 1907. Large crowds turned out to watch the soldiers in full dress uniform march from their barracks in Fulford Road to the Minster. Such parades were a popular annual event from their inception in 1892, by Dean Purey-Cust to celebrate the relief of Khartoum, to the last one in 1939.

The unveiling ceremony of the Green Howard's monument near Skeldergate Bridge in memory of those from the regiment lost in the Boer War. It was performed by Major-General Sir Leslie Rundle in May 1904. This monument and the one in Duncombe Place together commemorate the 1,320 Yorkshire lives lost in the war.

Soldiers line Farndale Street at the funeral of S.S. Batchelor of the 18th Hussars in February 1906. Some of the soldiers of the Princess of Wales Regiment hold wreaths while further down the road stand the Yorkshire Hussars, recognisable by the white plumes in their caps.

Funeral of S S M Batchelor

A close-up of the funeral parade. It must have been a stunning spectacle. The Scots Grey beating the drum would have cut a dash wearing his large busby, blue trousers with yellow braid and red tunic. Behind him sits a Green Howard astride a well-groomed horse decorated with gleaming harnesses.

Soldiers march over Skeldergate Bridge. After the outbreak of war in 1914, recruiting offices were set up in the city and large numbers of men enrolled. In August 1914, the knavesmire became a vast camp of artillery, cavalry and infantry soldiers. The regiments raised in York were sent to the front in 1914 and 1915.

The unveiling, on 14 June 1924, of the North Eastern Railway's monument to their 2,236 employees killed in the First World War. The memorial was designed by Edwin Lutyens and he had intended the wings to extend out further by cutting into the ramparts. After protests they were scaled down to keep the city walls intact.

Peace celebrations in Moss Street in August 1919. With 1,441 York men slain as well as 9 killed in the zeppelin raids on York in 1916, there was every cause to celebrate victory and peace. Street parties were held throughout the city in the summer folowing the November armistice.

A meeting of the civil defence unit of Holgate Ward in 1939. On the back row in gas masks are, from left to right: Alf Hudson, Walt Scaife, Henry Russling, George Wright, Jim Bailey, Dick Byworth, Bill Watson, Charlie Edwards. Middle row: D. Carriss, Stan Batters, Edwin Clark, Jess Smith, Albert Emerson (sadly killed in an air raid), John Brayshaw, Mrs Hearfield, Mrs Jowson, Peter Jowson, Mrs Clara Hudson, -?-, Mr Hunter, Fred Woods. Front row: Doris Byworth, Miss Byworth, Miss Byworth, Peggy Fost, David Hudson, Joe Boyes, ? Sharpe, -?-, Mrs Watson.

The Air Raid Patrol team at Rowntree's factory in 1941 – fully equipped and ready for action.

The scene in York Cemetery following the first air raid strike on York on 11 August 1940. There were 2 serious casualties and 69 houses suffered extensive damage. The impact of the blast caused glass damage to 153 houses. York had witnessed 11 air strikes by the end of the war and the air raid sirens had sounded over the city 138 times.

The cleaning up operation starts at St Mary's Convent in Micklegate after the Baedeker raid of 29 April 1942. Five sisters were killed in a night that resulted in the death of 71 men, women and children across the city. The damage to houses and buildings was extensive but remarkably the Minster and many of the historic sites were unscathed, although the roof of the medieval guildhall was completely destroyed.

The Queen inspects the troops of the Second Infantry Division at Imphal Barracks on 16 May 1983. The infantry barracks have survived, though their name has changed, but the cavalry barracks closed in the 1970s and now the police station occupies the site.

## *Seven*

# York's villages

A rural idyll. Osbaldwick village green in 1900, long before it was joined to York by continuous rows of houses.

A delightful picture of children running away from the camera in Nether Poppleton, 1908. It was taken by William Hayes, a talented and prolific York photographer. His brother, Thomas, was the village sub-postmaster, so William was a frequent visitor. Here he has captured a vivid reminder of Nether Poppleton at the turn of the century.

Children dance around the maypole on the green at Nether Poppleton, *c.* 1908. The maypole still stands and the May Day custom has recently been revived.

Children play in a traffic-free street in Nether Poppleton, *c.* 1905. In 1901 the population of the village was only 267 but it had its own station and, in 1908, it also had a branch of the Yorkshire Penny Bank which opened every Monday evening between 6.30 and 7p.m. in the elementary school.

Nether Poppleton from the air in the early 1980s. No longer a small village, by 1991 its population had expanded to 1,500. The early village with its triangular green and the cluster of houses around it contrasts vividly with the linear design of the new housing estates.

Horses pull carts loaded with timber in Heslington in the 1930s. At this time Heslington was an archetypal English village. Lord Deramore was the principal landowner and Lord of the Manor and he owned Heslington Hall. There was a parish church dedicated to St Paul, two Methodist chapels and a school. It also had a post office, a shop, a blacksmith and two pubs.

Heslington in the 1930s. The height of the straw loaded on the cart seems incredible! The 1936 directory lists one threshing machine owner in Heslington. He must have been a very busy man at this time of the year.

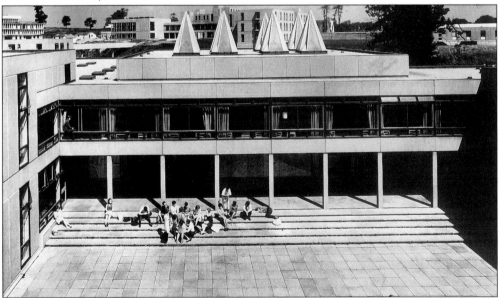

The arrival of the university at Heslington has transformed the village. The first campus buildings were opened in 1965 and it has continued to flourish. Heslington now heaves with students and staff during term time and must be the only village in England to have three major banks in its Main Street!

Skelton, c. 1900. The horse and cart wait outside the post office, often the hub of village life. Before the communications revolution, post offices were the main instrument for contact with the outside world.

Main Street in Strensall, c. 1900. It is little changed today, apart from the two cottages in the foreground which have been replaced by modern bungalows.

125

New Earswick, 1902-1918. This village was created by Joseph Rowntree in 1902. It followed on from Seebohm Rowntree's study of poverty in York, published in 1901, and it was planned to avoid the squalor of the working class slums he had exposed. Where the slums were characterised by narrow, dark, cramped terraces with no sanitation, the houses of the new village had gardens, upstairs bathrooms and were built in short curving rows with plenty of trees and open spaces.

The gardening class at New Earswick Primary School, 1912-1918. Before the school was built in 1912, the children had to leave the village to attend Haxby Road School. Fresh air was obviously felt to be good for the constitution with the wide open windows and the inclusion of gardening in the curriculum.

Haxby from St Mary's church gates in the mid-1950s. In the 1940s and '50s, Haxby was still a farming community and supported nine working farms. Times were changing however. By 1972, Bell's Garage had been demolished and Haxby Shopping Centre opened on the site to cater for the growing number of people moving into housing estates built on land that had previously been farmed.

A performance of the Haxby Mummers Play in 1922. It was traditionally acted out in the village every Plough Monday, which was the first Monday in January, and is also known as the Plough Stotts Play. Mummers plays are an ancient custom dating back to pagan times and represent the triumph of life over death, light over darkness and good over evil. There were four characters representing three of the seasons and the devil. Here the doctor (spring) is reviving the king (summer) who has been slain by the two villains (winter and beelzebub) who look on while holding their deadly weapons - two cooking pans!